VIKING
TWITTER ADS

Chapter 1:

Intro to Twitter Ads

What is Twitter?

Twitter is an incredibly powerful online news and social networking service. It's in a unique league of it's own due to several features that set it apart from other social networking platforms like Facebook, LinkedIn, and GooglePlus. Firstly, one of the main functions and uses of Twitter is as a news/events broadcasting channel. In many ways it's more like a news ticker than a social networking platform (albeit a news ticker where you get to choose what news you want to hear about by choosing who you follow). In fact, it's become a must-have resource for news networks and journalists who want to stay in the know about anything newsworthy in their areas. Journalists make up almost 25% of all verified Twitter accounts. Secondly, Twitter is all about short burst broadcasts. All posts consist of tiny bite sized messages, called Tweets, of 140 characters or less, or some combination of video/images and text. Users can broadcast and receive these messages via SMS, Mobile App, and the Twitter website interface.

Interaction with these posts can take the form of replies, likes, and retweets, with the latter being the ultimate sign of a successful tweet. For businesses and organizations, Twitter is used not only as a place to network and broadcast news, but also as a way to keep audiences updated about content published elsewhere. For example, some businesses primarily use Twitter as the "hey look" step in their content marketing plan, in which they simply Tweet every time they publish a new blog post on their website or a new video to their YouTube channel.

Bottom line: Twitter is a powerful, "short & sweet" social broadcasting platform that can play a very significant and positive role in any business' online marketing strategy.

Why Advertise on Twitter?

Advertising on Twitter could be one of the most impactful decisions you make in your business' online marketing strategy. Why? Because of the shear numbers, for starters. There are well over 300 Million active users on Twitter (nope, not a typo) and that's nothing compared to the total created accounts which is sitting at over 1.3 Billion (yes, with a "b"). Of that gargantuan amount, around half, 550 million, actually ever Tweet and another 500 million visit the site each month to read tweets and news without logging into their accounts. One-third of all US social media users are on Twitter and 80% of active users access the site via mobile. These days, anyone who is anyone is on Twitter, including over 80% of the world's leaders.

So that's all well and good from a purely personal perspective. Clearly the numbers are there. But what about business? Why should you market and advertise there? Well, if it's any indication, 65.8% of US businesses with 100+ employees are marketing on Twitter. 58% of the world's top brands have built and maintained enormous Twitter followings (100K or more). And how active are all these businesses on Twitter? 92% of them Tweet more than once per day, nearly half of them (42%) Tweet up to 5 times per day, and 20% of them go crazy and Tweet up to 10 times each day. Yeah, there's a good bet that these companies have a very good reason for putting so much marketing energy into Twitter.

So the businesses and companies are clearly on board. But what do consumers think? Well, the average Twitter user follows 5 companies and 80% of them have mentioned a brand or business in a Tweet. 54% of consumers on Twitter reported that they have taken action in response to seeing brands mentioned in Tweets (e.g. Retweeting, going to the brand's website, searching for the brand, etc). To finally drive the point home, Twitter revealed in 2016 that total paid ad engagements had grown a whopping 208% year-on-year. Yikes.

So, to conclude, the question clearly isn't whether or not you should be advertising on Twitter. The question is: What are you waiting for?

Chapter 2:
Establishing Goals

Establishing marketing goals is critical to the success of your Twitter advertising. Countless entrepreneurs and businesses have setup a Twitter presence, made a few posts and ads, and then let it sit untouched for months or even years. This is usually due to a lack or absence of goals. Also, your goals are will help you determine everything from your campaign objective to your budgeting and bidding. So before you even begin establishing any sort of Twitter ad strategy, you need to establish clear advertising goals.

Your goals should be specific, measurable, and attainable. They can be long term, short term, or a mix of both. Deadlines and milestones can be helpful as well. "I want to increase my Twitter following" would be an example of a bad goal that will likely result in your advertising efforts petering out after a while because there are no specific milestones. "I want to gain 1,000 followers by New Years" is an example of a good goal. It's specific, measurable, and certainly attainable. Below are some examples of the various goal categories you might be interested in.

Traffic to Website (Sales, Leads, Content)

Probably one of the most popular goals of Twitter Advertising is to funnel Twitter traffic back to your own web properties. After all, most businesses don't do business "on" Twitter, per se. You're leveraging Twitter ads to obtain traffic and convert that Twitter traffic into brand-followers, leads, prospects, and customers. So maybe your goal is to get people to a landing page with a free offer where they can subscribe to your list and become a lead. Maybe they're being sent to a sales page or an eCommerce store. Maybe you just want to do some content marketing and send them to your blog so you can cookie them with a pixel and create a warm retargeting audience that you can advertise to later on. Maybe you're a brick and mortar local business and you want to increase actual foot traffic into your store, restaurant, or office by offering a coupon or announcing a sale or new menu item. Whatever the case, the end goal for a lot of businesses will likely be bringing Twitter traffic AWAY from Twitter and over to their own web properties or physical locations.

Gain More Followers (aka Twitter as Autoresponder)

In this goal category, your aim is to build a large number of Twitter followers. The reason we also refer to this as "Twitter as Autoresponder" is because the main sought-after benefit here is to increase the number of people who will see your Tweets in their Twitter Feeds. In this sense, your Tweets become similar to sending out email broadcasts via your autoresponder. If you grow a large enough Twitter following, this can be very beneficial and if your content is engaging enough to get a lot of traction in the form of likes, replies, and retweets, you can significantly increase the range of your organic reach into people's newsfeeds to a point where your organic Tweets are almost as far reaching and effective as your paid ads!

PR and Company News

Sponsored Tweets can be a great way to enhance your brand's public image and share a little about your company culture. People enjoy seeing "the other side" of a business. What happens on the inside? Did you recently promote/hire a new executive and want to publicly welcome him/her to the team? Did somebody in the office make a funny video about donut day? Did you guys recently sponsor a charity event or volunteer at a local food pantry? Do you want to share a funny blooper reel from a recent sales video? Even Tweeting inspirational images and videos about popular or noble causes and movements that have nothing to do with your company can help to associate your identity with feelings of goodwill. There are countless things you can use sponsored Tweets for that will enhance your PR and generate positive vibes about your company.

Brand Awareness

Another goal that's less thought about might be spreading brand awareness and recognition. If you're just starting out, there's a good chance your brand might be in need of a jump start. If nobody's ever heard of you, a great way to increase recognition is to simply create and share unique, helpful, or entertaining content and get your name, logo, and overall brand identity in front of as many people as possible as many times as possible. If this is your goal, you want to avoid being salesy in the beginning. Ensure you're focused almost entirely on Twitter Ads consisting of helpful, relevant, or entertaining content that simply gets your name, brand, logo, or image in front of people.

Market research

A hugely beneficial goal of Twitter Advertising is market research. If you're just starting your business or going down a new path, Twitter ads and sponsored Tweets can be an excellent way to learn more about your audience and your market. This can be done in a structured way with things like surveys and questionnaires, or in a less structured way by simply engaging with your audience, asking questions, and so on. Ultimately, your goal should be to come up with one or two ideal customer avatars that you can then base your marketing and product development on.

This was a pretty good summary of potential Twitter advertising goals, but yours might be slightly different. Whatever they are, ensure that they are specific, measurable, and attainable and put them down in writing before moving on to ad creation.

Chapter 3:
Ad Campaigns

So, hopefully by now you've established your Twitter Advertising goals. Now it's time to create a campaign. And the first step is deciding on a campaign type.

Campaign Types

There are six types of Twitter Ad Campaigns, also referred to as "objectives". These include Website Traffic ads, Twitter Following ads, Tweet Engagement ads, Video View ads, Brand Awareness ads, and App Install ads. Depending on your goals, you might end up using just one, a few, or even all of these ad types at some point. We'll take a closer look at each ad type right now.

Website Clicks

One of the most common Twitter ad types is the "website clicks" ad. This is more or less exactly what it sounds like. Use this ad type to send traffic from Twitter to your website, a squeeze page, sales page, eCommerce store, or a piece of content like a blog post or article. For your ad creative you can use either a "website card" or other media or even just a textual Tweet. Ideally, you'll want to include a very clear call to action in your ad to encourage people to not only click, but also to follow through with certain actions on your website or page. With website clicks, you're setting your bidding and budget in accordance with how many clicks you get to your website. Any other benefits you gain from this ad such as followers, retweets, likes, and so on are completely free.

Website click ads work great when combined with conversion tracking. Simply place your Twitter website "tag" code (the name Twitter uses for their tracking pixels) on the appropriate page for the type of action you're tracking. For example, if you're collecting leads, place your code on the thank you page. The number of people tracked as arriving on that page tells you how many people filled out your lead form. We'll discuss more about conversion tracking and analysis later. For now, just know it's a good idea to have a website tag on as many of your pages as possible so you can make use of that information later on.

Tweet Engagement Ads

Tweet engagement campaigns are an excellent way to boost your reach and the number of people interacting with and sharing your content. You can either create an ad creative for this purpose or you can choose to use an existing organic Tweet. Basically, a Tweet engagement ad campaign promotes these Tweets to a bigger, targeted audience that you otherwise wouldn't reach organically. Rather than painstakingly trying to organically network your way in front of the perfect audience on Twitter, you can have any Tweet appear in front of your ideal target audience right in their Twitter feeds.

These Tweets look and behave exactly like normal Tweets except that they have a small label on them that says "promoted". This native look and feel really helps increase the amount of engagements you can expect to receive. In the case of Tweet engagement campaigns, you're basically paying Twitter for every time a person interacts with your Tweet in any way. This includes retweets, replies, likes, and pretty much any other interaction a person may have with your promoted Tweet.

Increase Followers

Twitter followers can be super valuable for your business. Unlike Facebook, where the percentage of your followers who see your organic posts is very small, with Twitter, your followers can pretty much be expected to see all your Tweets. For that reason alone, the Increase Followers Ad Type can be very beneficial. Customers who follow you on Twitter are much more likely to become customers and advocates of your brand. According to Twitter's own research, 75% of consumers feel better about small and medium-sized businesses after following them on Twitter and 69% have purchased from a business because of Twitter content once or more. This campaign type promotes your actual Twitter account, rather than individual Tweets, to a target audience that you think might be interested in your brand. It does so by featuring your account in places like the "Who to Follow" panel and their "Home" timeline. In this case, you'll be paying Twitter based on instances of people choosing to follow you. This can be an easy and relatively inexpensive way to accelerate your follower growth and significantly boost your organic reach.

Brand Awareness Ads

Awareness campaigns can be incredibly helpful in getting your brand name or identity in front of as many eyeballs as possible and ultimately drive better awareness for your business. This can be especially useful when you're a newer brand and you're looking for a quick boost in name recognition within your target market, niche, or industry. The ad, in this case, can be any typical promoted Tweet, meaning text-only or text and media, but the real difference is in what you're paying for. Rather than paying for specific actions taken by users on your Tweets, you're paying for impressions. An impression is any time a Tweet is made visible in someone's newsfeed.

The great thing about this model is that impressions are dirt cheap. One thousand impressions will typically cost you anywhere from a few dollars to $12 depending on things like targeting. The downside is that impressions come and go very quickly and don't necessarily produce direct ROI or results. A person could literally scroll or swipe past your Tweet, barely noticing it, and that would count as one impression. If your goal is to get your brand in front of as many people as possible in a short amount of time, then this would be fine, because people would at least be getting exposed to your logo or image, even if they aren't stopping to learn more. Just don't expect a ton of engagements or clicks from these Tweets (although you'll get a little bit and it doesn't cost you extra.

Video Views (aka "Promoted Video")

Video view ads are exactly what they sound like. You're exposing your video to as much of your target audience as possible and paying Twitter for each time a person watches that video. This is very useful because videos on Twitter are shown to drive the highest recall and emotional connection of any digital platform, according to Business.Twitter.com. Another recent addition that makes this advertising tool even more powerful is the auto-play feature, which causes your video ad to automatically start playing with no sound as users scroll past it in their timelines. This dramatically boosts interactions and views.

Since you're lining Twitter's pockets, they allow you more freedom with videos than organic video Tweets. File size can be huge, but they recommend you keep it under 1GB. Maximum length is 2 minutes and 20 seconds, but you're allowed to ask them directly for up to 10 minute length and if you qualify, they'll allow it. Frame rate should be 29.97 or higher (they're trying to keep Twitter timelines pretty, of course) and videos ideally should be at least 720p resolution or higher for that nice crisp look. Twitter recommends you have a good CTA in the textual part of your Tweet, namely a CTA explaining why they should watch your video. They also recommend you get the meat and potatoes of your message out clearly in the first 15 seconds and keep the rest of your message short and sweet.

WARNING: Twitter considers any instance of auto-play in the timeline at 50% view lasting 2 seconds or more to be a chargeable video view. This means you'll be paying even if people don't unmute or click to enlarge the video. This shouldn't discourage you, but just be aware of it when you're establishing your budget and bidding.

App Installs and App Re-engagement

One very powerful feature of Twitter advertising is it's app install/engage ad objective. This only applies to you if you have a mobile app of some sort. If you do, you can create a promoted Tweet that actually connects to your app on the app store and pay Twitter for each time a person installs your app onto their device. Beyond that, if you're looking to get more people to open that app later on, you can create Twitter ads that cause the app to open up on their device. This can be a great way to keep your mobile audience thinking about your brand or engaging with your software or content. You can choose to pay Twitter for clicks to install or for actual completed installations, and of course, for clicks to open the app in the case of app re-engagement.

So, now that you've got a handle on creating Twitter ads, how do you ensure they're performing as well as they could and how do you capitalize on that traffic you just paid good money for? That's what we'll be covering in the next section.

Chapter 4:

Analyze, Optimize, Retarget

One reason a lot of independent advertisers give up on Twitter ads is because their first experience is underwhelming. Somewhere inside, maybe unconsciously, they were expecting their first campaign to make them millionaires overnight and when that doesn't happen, they give up. This is a huge mistake! Twitter ads can work wonders for your business. The trick is to analyze, optimize, and Retarget!

Analysis and Stats

Twitter has an awesome analytics dashboard and plenty of useful data to help you track and analyze the performance of your ad campaigns. From your Twitter advertising dashboard you can see things like impressions, engagements, views, clicks, conversion rates, and (maybe most importantly) costs. When you compare all this data against your ad creative, bidding strategy, and audience targeting, you should have a pretty good idea of your ads performance. Once you've taken a look at your performance, it's time to optimize.

Campaign Optimization

The idea behind optimizing your Twitter ad campaign is to basically tweak various aspects of it, test the results of those tweaks against a baseline (e.g. the original campaign), and watch what happens. If the tweak produced an improvement, keep it! That tweaked version now becomes the new norm and it's time to choose another aspect or element to tweak.

For example, let's say you've got an ad campaign for firefighter-themed t-shirt sales designed to direct traffic to your eCommerce store. You've got an image in your Tweet of a firefighter silhouetted in front of some scary flames and a textual CTA saying "Free Firefighter T-shirts!". The ad is performing worse than you had hoped. For your first attempt at optimization, you might change the CTA and make it a little more wordy: "Grab your free firefighter t-shirt and celebrate our nation's first responders!". After implementing that tweak, you notice that your click through rate increases and cost per click goes down a little. That just became your new baseline. Next, you remove the dark silhouette image and replace it with a bright flat tabletop background with one of your Firefighter T-shirts spread out on it. Big suprise: your performance improves.

The big thing to keep in mind for this process is that you only want to make one change at a time, otherwise you won't know which change caused the improvement. This can be done all with the same ad, although it would be best to simply discontinue the baseline one and then make the tweaks to successive cloned versions so that you retain each version and can look back and analyze the differences. Also, make sure you don't rush to judgement on each variation. You'll want to have at least 25-50 conversions or actions (and I mean AT LEAST) before you give a final thumbs up or down to each tweak or variation.

Once you've tweaked your ads to perfection, you'll want to move on to optimizing your funnel and capitalizing on your visitors.

Tracking Pixel (aka Website Tag)

The first step to tracking and capitalizing on your traffic is to install your website tag code (the thing everyone else in the world calls a tracking pixel). You can get this from inside your ad account (use the "universal website tag" option). Place this tag on every relevant page of your website. This should include your squeeze pages, your thank you pages, your sales pages, your checkout pages and order forms, your upsell pages and pretty much every page in your funnel. You should also put this in your members area welcome page. This way, you'll be able to track and analyze the way your traffic flows through your whole customer experience and where in the funnel your customers are stopping. This way you can tweak the pages in question to try to improve their conversion rates. This also gives you a solid idea of how much money you're making from your ad campaign and which parts of your funnel are producing the most revenue.

Retargeting Audiences

Once you've got your pixel (tag code) where you need it, it's time to start retargeting. Retargeting is done by creating custom audiences based on user behavior across your pages. The most basic form of retargeting is to simply retarget everyone who has visited your web property. In this case, all you care about is that the audience is "warm", which means that they have now been exposed to your brand or site and are at least somewhat familiar with you. A more advanced form of retargeting, however, is action-based retargeting. In this case you create a custom audience based on pages someone visited and/or didn't visit, and you then custom tailor an ad message to them.

One example might be for people who did land on your squeeze page, but did not land on your thank you page. You know these are people who didn't grab your free gift or opt-in, so you can retarget them reminding them to grab that free offer and why they'll like it. Another example might be upsell reminders. In this case, you'd create a custom audience of people who landed on your upsell page, meaning they bought the initial front-end product, but did not land on the next page after the upsell (whether that be a thanks page or another upsell page). This means you can follow them around Twitter with a tailored message inviting them to upgrade or offering a coupon. This same method can be applied to the eCommerce realm simply by placing your code on your order page and also on the post-purchase/success page and targeting those who hit the former but not the latter.

So there you have it. A clear strategy for leveraging paid ads on Twitter. But none of it will count for anything if you don't apply what you've learned. Make sure either you or your team start implementing what you've learned right away using the battle plan below.

Battle Plan

Step 1: Establish your big-picture Twitter advertising goals and ensure they're specific, measurable, and attainable.

Step 2: Choose an appropriate Ad type or "objective".

Step 3: Make your targeting and budget decisions for your first ad in accordance with the goals you established at the beginning.

Step 4: Design an ad creative that's eye catching and engaging.

Step 5: Analyze your performance after getting at least around 25-50 conversions.

Step 6: Start tweaking and optimizing your campaign to boost performance.

www.ingramcontent.com/pod-product-compliance
Lightning Source LLC
Chambersburg PA
CBHW040931210326
41597CB00030B/5264